ALL
for my
GOOD

The Caged Princess

Trenesha S. Boyd

ISBN 979-8-88685-492-3 (paperback)
ISBN 979-8-88685-493-0 (digital)

Copyright © 2022 by Trenesha S. Boyd

All rights reserved. No part of this publication may be reproduced, distributed, or transmitted in any form or by any means, including photocopying, recording, or other electronic or mechanical methods without the prior written permission of the publisher. For permission requests, solicit the publisher via the address below.

Christian Faith Publishing
832 Park Avenue
Meadville, PA 16335
www.christianfaithpublishing.com

Printed in the United States of America

The Arrest

It was October 17, 1993, and there was a lot going on in the build-ings (projects). A few people had got shot, fights were jumping off, and I immediately headed to my parents' house for the night with the kids. I had no idea what would happen next; be prepared, it was an experience that would last for a lifetime.

The following day, which was the eighteenth, I was asleep for most of the day. It had to be around 5:00 or 6:00 p.m. when my dad came in to wake me up. He never said that the police were at the door, and I honestly thought they had questions about the shootout the day before. As I walked to the door, I can hear my dad asking me, "What was going on?" I didn't know at the time.

The detective whispered in my ear because he also noticed my two small children peeking around the corner, and named a few indi-viduals who I had been running with and committing crimes; they had been in custody already. I found out later that people were trying to contact me, but I never answered my phone. It was at this point that I knew this was more serious than my original thoughts, and I had no clue of what I had gotten myself into.

When I arrived at the police station, I saw a few of the guys who were with me, and they were going in and out of a room, which I later found out was a lineup. The detectives kept asking me questions about different places that had been robbed, but I kept my cool, tell-ing them that I could not remember. I knew inside that whoever was talking had to be with us quite often because the detectives knew so much information about everyone's role in the acts.

I was handcuffed to a door where everyone could see me and that included the witnesses which I knew was unfair, especially when it came time for me to be identified by the witnesses. The funny thing about this particular lineup was that it was subjective, and they knew I was the suspect in a lineup with older women with wigs on and miniskirts. I'm sure none of them fit the description of the woman they were looking for (a twenty-three-year-old black female).

I still had no clue of what was really going on. We had discussed jail one time when the guys said I would not get any hard time and would get probation because I did not have a criminal record. They did share that they would be sent down the river because of the previous arrest. I never knew women went to jail. I watched *Prisoner: Cell Block H* and just thought it was another show, not real at all.

When we were being transported from the police station to Cook County Jail, I just knew that I would be getting out soon, but boy was I in for a surprise. I had been sheltered by my parents all of my life, and I was totally ignorant as to how this system was set up or even the injustices that go on. My aunt who worked in the drug program was in the bullpen when I made it to Cook County Jail, and she promised me she would get me on the drug unit.

I was like, "I don't need to be on the drug unit," even though I did because I was so angry and beat down that I needed some help—mentally, physically, and emotionally. It was never about the drug but more about me not being able to cope with life, hurt, and pain that I did not realize had such an effect on me. When I got into my cell after being processed for what seemed like forever, I was finally put on a tier with the general population. It was so late by this time; my roommate was sleeping when I came into the cell.

The next day when I met my roommate, I was very confused because before I knew it, I was saying, "I did not know this was co-ed." Yes, she looked just like a guy, and at that point, I knew I had to go to Gateway immediately. I screamed through the chuckhole for the guard to contact my aunt. There was no way I was staying there. This was my first reaction, but after meeting and talking to my very first roommate for a couple of days until I was transferred, she was a nice and caring person. She knew that I was nervous because all of this was new to me being this was my first arrest.

I did get in trouble one time before when my daughter's godmother was being watched at her job, and she did not charge me for all of the items I had purchased. We were taken to the station and let out. The end result was supervision, and I thought that was so crazy; but again, I was not raised around any criminal activity, and I looked at it as we got busted, not a crime.

I completed my supervision, and that was it; that was nothing compared to this. My roommate made me comfortable, and our friendship grew over time. I saw her come back and forth in the County as well as Dwight. I could not believe that the people I was seeing on the news were right before my eyes. I guess people could have said the same thing about me as well.

My family saw me on the news too. This just felt like a dream I was stuck in, and everyone who I talked to was always talking about what each case carried which was six to thirty years. If I did not catch on to anything else, I always knew that this was serious trouble. There were other causes, but that all comes later. So for the next couple of weeks, we were going back and forth to court. I could not sleep because reality was setting in.

Throughout my teenage and young adult years, I would find myself saying, "If there is really a God, why is there so much violence and hatred? I was raised a Catholic, and my brother was a Jehovah's Witness; other than that, no one in my family was religious or spiritual that I knew of.

Anyway, it was during the first week of being locked up that God came to me, showing me the times He had spared my life and let me know that He had done it again by removing me from society before something terrible would have happened. I had received a little Bible from one of the clergies who would come to visit the tiers. I started having Bible study with a clergy member. She would come get me, and I would study the Bible and ask many questions.

I can remember on December 29, 1993, at 10:15 a.m., I had accepted Christ. I felt really good, and for once, I felt so special knowing that God had been sheltering and protecting me my entire life. I felt special, and this new-found love I had for God would carry me for the heavy burden that I would be enduring.

Many people look at jail or prison as a negative experience; as for me, it saved my life! I had a few bad or sad moments, but nothing compares to the consequences that I could have been faced with had I not been arrested. I had to learn how to do the time and not let the time do me whatever that might look like. I still could not believe after my loving life and great upbringing that I would find myself in a jail cell.

County Blues

My parents were always present in court and for visits. After every court appearance, we would put the *I love you* sign up, which was at the time the strength I needed to carry on until the next court date. In the earlier days of my arrest, I wouldn't always know the dates because they were putting us in any similar cases, which included the Brown's Chickens murders, which we had *nothing* to do with!

My family would bring my kids to visit, and even though my baby boy was two years old, it had an effect on him that I hated to think about. I wondered how this two-year-old would turn his back on me and refuse to come into the visiting room. Some people might think that children don't know certain things, but I promise, my baby boy did, and it reflected on his behavior for the next couple of years.

My parent shared that the whole separation from my children was not that good, especially from my baby boy because he was spoiled rotten and familiar to his older sister; he didn't say much and would sit in my dad's window waiting for her to come from daycare. It was hard on everyone because not only did my children have to readjust, but so did my immediate family.

I never thought about these consequences and the effect that they would have on my family. To be honest, I don't think I was thinking at all. I never worried about the children being neglected or mistreated because I had the *perfect family* full of love. I knew that my children would be good but never thought of the mental or emotional effect that my drastic separation would have on them mentally. It was all about me, and it took some time and my growing relationship with God to see the truth from others' eyes. They had already been exposed to things that I never would have thought of as a child, things that if I had known better could have taken them away, not for neglect or anything but for the environment and people that I allowed around them.

It was not normal, and sometimes love can be blind; and due to my ignorance and sheltered upbringing, I probably didn't look at life as others did. I always saw the good in people and had no idea that the reality was that I had been protected by God, and He surrounded me with the best family. They were loving and supportive, and they worked together as a team to get whatever was needed to be done.

Shortly after I got locked up, my dad was diagnosed with cirrhosis of the liver and needed a transplant. I could not believe that this was really happening, and I was sitting here in the county jail fighting for my life while my dad was burdened with a medical crisis, adding to the list of stress in my family's life. I felt so powerless, and I knew that the only thing that I could offer was my continued prayers and remain positive about the entire ordeal.

Thank God for saving me in the nick of time. Things might not have turned out very well for me with the path I was traveling down. I must admit that it was not looking good for a sister. I had just gotten into the gang, drugs, and criminal activities not even for two years, and God had snatched me out quickly. I am not confused about how I was on a death wish, hurting on the inside and rebelling outwardly!

I remember when I was angry and began to shut down, and my parents did send me to a therapist. I was not honest and did not share anything concrete, and even until this day, I believe that I could have prevented a lot of unwanted pain if I had just been honest about how I was feeling. When I think back, I can see where God was sparing my life and working everything together for my good! At first, my family tried to keep my dad's illness from me; but one day, they came to visit, and he was already a slim man. The sickness did not help, and his stomach was very big due to the fluids not being processed as they should.

Our liver's primary function is to break down blood, activate enzymes, and metabolize fats, proteins, and carbohydrates just to name a few. My dad was in the stage where he would not live without a transplant. I couldn't believe my eyes that in such a short period of time, this could be happening; but for some reason, my faith in God only began to grow stronger.

I stood solely on God's word in my situation as well as in my dad's. My brother and sister-in-law always came to see me as well and helped with the kids, especially when dad got sick. He had so many scheduled appointments, and he had to be prepared for the day when he got the call for a liver. They even gave him a pager that whenever they found a match, he would have a certain amount of time to get to the hospital.

I had developed the faith of a mustard seed and met some wonderful people who were placed in my life to plant seeds of faith and trust in God. The support we had for one another was priceless. Some of these relationships would be for a reason, season, or a lifetime. I remember one day, two good friends came to visit me, and one of them said, "I hate to say it, but I told you that you stuck out like a sore thumb, and why was I hanging with the people in the first place?"

Everyone always thought that with my upbringing, support, and education, my life would have turned out much different. Unfortunately, God had other plans! Rather, He allows us to make our own decisions and eventually will redirect the path. Many people wanted to point the finger to bad influences that I was involved or hanging with, but for the most part, I had always taken my own weight. I might have been ignorant of a lot of things in the real world, but what I did know was the difference between right and wrong.

In this case, I made bad decisions that caused harm to myself and others. They were also coming to see how much my bond was, and that's when I found out that I did not have a bond, and they had named me the *mastermind* with another person. I was the only female on a case with four males, and I am the only one who did not have a bond. (Talking about things that make you go hmm?)

Thank God for our relationship because it was at that point that I knew I had to go through the storm and sit it out. I was never going to *cop out*, and I just felt they were being a little hard, especially with no weapon or really anything credible as it related to me. I was there to fight! It seemed like for months. I was going back and forth to court and kept getting continuances. I had no knowledge of the judicial system; no one in my family went to jail except one uncle at this time. So besides TV, who knew the truth about what happens behind bars?

I was not giving up on anything. My family had a lawyer who was pretty good, and he had actually shared with my family that the ten years they were offering was a good deal, and he did not bother to go further with the case, so I eventually was given a lawyer from the multiple units of codefendants.

She was a pretty smart lady who found out quickly that I was not an ordinary person, and I would not be taking any time. We had many arguments on my stance because she thought it was a good deal as well, considering she would not be the one doing time. I am sure that my family also agreed with the lawyers as well and really thought I was losing my mind. One thing about us was that we stuck together; and even if they were scared that I would get the book thrown at me, they supported my choices.

I guess it was over a year by now, and three of my codefendants had taken their time without going to trial. I was upset because I really felt if we would have stuck together, things might have turned out differently, and we all could have gone home. That is just wishful thinking because no jury or judge was just going to let us walk; we would have had to beat every case we were charged with.

Peace on P1

After being transferred to the Gateway unit, there was an instant difference in the units. They had coffee, snacks, and an organized structure. I couldn't believe that that unit as well as Q1 was a part of Division 4. Gateway had orientation with a list of rules and regulations; we had to remember the Gateway Philosophy which I still remember to this day and actually stayed with me. Gateway gave me a lot of structure, and it made me work my way up to Head of House, considering I had been locked up so long at this time. I was there for at least six months. Around the same time, three of the guys on the case were saying that they were going to take the time offered and run with it.

I was just not willing to give up without a fight and was willing to stay as long as I had to. It was approaching a year, and I remember clearly having a court date in October. When I got back on the tier, it was after 5:00 p.m. If I did not catch the officers before the shift changed, we were stuck in the bullpen until the next shift felt like coming to pick us up. Later on, that night, I called my brother like I usually do after every court date in Cook County as well as Maywood. My sister-in-law answered and shared with me that my dad was at the hospital because he received a liver donor. What a miracle from God. Who would have ever thought things would move so fast. God was showing me that He was looking out for my family at home too.

I knew the surgery would be several hours (twelve or more), so the only thing that I could really do was continue to pray. P1 was a close net unit, we prayed for one another, we fed one another, and we held one another accountable when it came to our relationships. I spoke with my mom the next day, and she informed me that my dad had a successful transplant, and his recovery process was going well. We never know how situations like this turned out, but my prayer, in this case, would be that his body would not reject the liver. It all worked together for his good for sure. Who would have thought that he would be blessed with a donor, and it would happen so soon?

In the meantime, I would continue to go to all of these continuances every month. Three of my codefendants got tired of the back-and-forth court dates until they decided to take the time offered before it was too late. I was left with one other codefendant who was never with us during the brief crime spree but somehow got caught up in our mess. So for the next year, I would keep going to court, believing that I was going home because I knew that the only person left was innocent, and there was no way that I would be convicted.

That entire case was shady, and it was God's will, not ours, that was being done. He was the wrong person from the very beginning, but because a witness identified him in a lineup, he had to stay and fight the case with me. It is mishaps like this that show me how unfair our justice system is. People are really guilty until proven innocent, and that is why so many people are in jails, prisons, or even are dead from everyone wanting to be right and taking the easy way out of investigations or even witnesses.

My trial was set for February of 1995, and I really believed that I was going home, especially since the individual who was charged with armed robbery was not with us, and I believed that he had a witness or an alibi for the day that he allegedly participated in a crime. I also felt that my God had saved me to go to trial and eventually be released. It was time for the trial, and the guards were used to me and my parents, and I was able to see my remaining codefendant. He told me that he was going to take eight years and was stressing out. I immediately told him that was the devil, and he was going home.

Jail can break the best of us, and it had taken a toll on LF. Besides, he was truly innocent and had nothing to do with the crimes that had been committed. It was at that point I knew that I would have to make a conscious decision in order to save an innocent person. My relationship with God had grown, and there was no way that I would not speak up for what was right even when my lawyer had informed me that once I testified, I would be admitting my guilt. When it came time for me to testify, I told on myself in hopes that another would go free. Even though the judge said I was not a credible witness, I am 90 percent sure that my testimony was a major factor in the *not-guilty* verdict for the man who witnesses stated held them at gunpoint, robbed them, and locked them in a freezer.

The trial went on for maybe three or four days on the day of the judge reading the verdict; something different took place. The judge started with my codefendant first, and my lawyer wrote on a piece of paper not guilty for him. I put my head down because I knew that meant I would be found guilty. When it came down to my sentence, the judge had received letters on my behalf from teachers, family, officers, Gateway staff, and friends. He gave me a pretty good speech and even acknowledged my parental and family support. He shared about his thoughts about track stars and swimmers being smart people, and then he said, whatever time you are sentenced to after pre-sentence investigation, he wanted me to get out and help others who get caught up in situations like mine.

As you might have picked up, I was found guilty! One good thing that came out of that was the judge let me get a visit with my parents, and that was the strength that I needed to carry on. I was so happy that the grief of losing did not compare to the love I felt from my parents' hugs and support. God did it again. He always gave me exactly what I needed in the nick of time. Who would think that all of the time I was thinking that my "innocent rappie" was there to set me free, I was actually there to make sure that he would go home after being locked up for almost two years?

Whatever God spared him from during that time was between them. When I returned to my tier, I shared the news with my friends and new-found family, and even though I had no clue what would happen, my prayers changed to, "Lord, let me get no more than ten years," since that was the offer in the beginning. I sort of felt that that would be the starting point even though I never had a background.

It was early in March 1995 and time for my sentencing; regardless of how things might have looked and the usual that if you take your case to trial and lose, the time will be doubled, I believed that God would work it all out for my good, and things would still work for my good. My prayers had also changed to running all my cases concurrently and Maywood agreeing with whatever Cook County sentenced me to. Even though this was one arrest, I had cases in two counties, which meant everyone needed to be on one accord.

My prayers had become specific. It seemed like those thirty days had passed by before I knew it, and my cell door would be unlocked for my final court date and sentencing if everything went right. This would be a bittersweet day in which I was so glad that I would no longer have to be stripped down in the bullpen like an animal, squatting and coughing to make sure I'm not smuggling anything in. This was the routine every time I went to court, which was a lot, especially in the beginning. The guards in the courtroom and even the judge were pretty nice to me after all of the court appearances; they saw the real me and the love I had for my family.

Right before we were being called up in front of the judge, my attorney came in and said they are doing a plea with the other cases as well. I didn't think of the other cases, but I had five more six–thirty-year cases which had to be addressed with this judge. I had three more cases. They had offered me the ten years with the other cases concurrent, and I just point-blank asked, "How many years will I be doing?" She told me three years and three months give or take. At this point, I had no other option but to accept the offer because it could have turned out much different.

Listening to jailhouse lawyers can have a person's mind all over the place, but trusting God never fails. Can you believe that I was happy for a ten-year sentence and thanking God? When I got in front of the judge, he asked did I have anything to say. My apology was to the court and victims but mainly to my family for putting them through all of this.

When a person gets locked up, their entire family, parents, children, and anyone attached to them are imprisoned as well. Just like I am being searched, waiting in lines, or being talked down on, my family was experiencing some of the same hardships, and they were free. Just attending every court date in two different places and visits was enough. There was so much going on outside, and yet my family still did everything they could to make me comfortable even in jail.

After it was all said and done, I still had to hope that the judge in Maywood would accept the deal as well because I had two cases out there. I think that court date was a couple of days after, so the prayer this time was for the cases to be run concurrently as well. When I got in front of the Maywood judge, he let me know that he was going to agree with the county judge but didn't really like it as evidence of him stating, "I must be getting soft!"

In my head, I was like, *What does that mean? Ten years is a lot of time!* So now, it was finally over, and I would be shipped off to Dwight within the next week or two to begin my sentence or rather finish it because I will be getting credit for all the time I was in the county.

Prison Bound

Well, it was a week after the verdict, and it was the night before I was being shipped to Dwight Correctional Center. The staff and peers on Gateway sent me off with a bang. I felt so much love. I had my closest friends who I had prayer with, and they gave me positive encouraging words as I transition to my next stop, which was state prison.

I had a special friend, an older lady G, who I sort of adopted as my mom and always had her back. She had was on a case with her sister who died in Cook County Jail, which left her to be charged with the case and sentenced for the crime. She never shared with us that she was found guilty, made a plea deal, or even she would be getting shipped as well; so when the guard unlocked our doors, I thought it was a mistake, or she maybe was serving breakfast. I never knew that she was being shipped too. It was a bittersweet moment because she had held in emotions of taking time and not sharing it with any of our group. She was always shy, and I believe that she did not want us to worry about her. If she felt guilty, it was only because of the devil playing with her thinking.

None of us was in any position to judge; we were all in the same place—jail! The great thing was that God kept us together, and we both were blessed to continue our program with Gateway. I used to laugh and say, "I've been in this program longer than I even used drugs, but the truth to the matter is that people usually use drugs, people, or things because of the way they feel, so I was exactly where I was supposed to be." I quickly adapted to the program down there, and before you know it, I was the Gateway Queen once again.

I was one who did not play about the rules or behaviors, and it showed in my actions. I was far from perfect, but one thing I have always been was being honest. I was able to attend college because I had a high school diploma. I attended Lewis University. The funny thing with all of this was that I thought everyone attended high school and had no clue what a GED was until I went to the county jail. I tutored people and helped them prepare for the test, and a lot of them did pass. I did the same in prison. I was always a helpful individual, and for the most part, I found out how blessed I had been with how I was raised by both of my parents, attended Catholic/private schools, and had so much family support and love even as I was going through this experience.

So many people automatically believe that an individual must have a hard, abusive childhood, or trauma-filled life. I am here to cancel out that theory that is consistently handed down in our communities, which usually confirms that a person usually experiences all of these negative events that lead a person down the wrong path. Not my story! I was so in love with my family, and we were so *perfect* that it totally devastated me when I found out that that was not the truth.

So that traumatic situation combined with an unhealthy relationship led to me making rash decisions and rebelling against things that I knew were not good for me. I wanted to make everyone hurt like I was hurting, especially my "phony family." My behavior did not change at once, but I slowly began to please others and fit in to places that I just didn't fit. I was mean, very angry, and unhappy for some time, but thank God I had my kids to keep me somewhat grounded.

Once I moved down the street, it all went downhill. I had a misconception about people and always found the good in everyone. It didn't take long before I noticed that my *fairy-tale* life had me totally confused as to what life was really about. I had been sheltered for my entire life, and even though I thought I knew a lot about life, I was much more ignorant and naïve than I had thought. I had created an image to the people that I eventually had to live up to. I never fit, but the loyalty and relationship that I saw from my parents allowed me to be very loyal and stay in something that I knew was not good for me; but because of the kids, I would do anything.

I felt family was everything and always did things focused on that even if that meant some things would turn out to be negative. God allowed me to take my personal responsibility for the choices I had made, beginning with taking a break from school once I graduated from the twelfth grade. It also allowed me to think about how selfish I really was when I thought about how my parents sacrificed a lot in order to give me and my brother the best upbringing possible.

God had always had my back, and things were working all for my good since birth. I was able to continue to stay in treatment working on my behaviors and thinking which was a good thing for me and Ma G. We stayed in the program for another six months before we moved into the general population, and shortly after that, we again were transferred to Dixon Correctional Center.

I couldn't believe it, but I knew that God needed me to look after her, and she would keep me focused. When we got to Dixon, we not only moved into the same unit, but we were also in the dorm room of eight together. I was so very grateful, and Ma G was just crying and thanking God because we had already been together for over two years. He saved me and put me around people that He knew would pour into me, plus God knew that Ma G would be diagnosed with cervical cancer. She had beautiful long hair in the beginning, but by the time her treatment was over, her head was bald.

I am so glad that I was given that assignment of making sure Ma G had all of the love and support from everyone around her, which made our life in prison much better. I was also the peacemaker and counselor. Whenever there were any issues or fights, they would come and get me, especially for one of my closest friends who was always beating someone up. Thank God that He delivered her from a lot of things as well. She was doing big things and taking things one day at a time.

The laundry room was my office space, and I loved helping people get to the root of their issues or just being a sounding board to listen. I always prayed and let God have His way, but I was never the judgmental type because we all fall short, and I had my share of shortcomings. I never shared their secrets, and I was told many things that were deep and very personal. While in Dixon, I attended Lewis University, and I obtained my associate's degree in the process. Time was winding down, and it was less than six months before my discharge date, and I couldn't wait. I had been waiting to hear back from my counselor to see if I would be eligible. Since I had a violent offense, they sometimes didn't give the good time to.

It was in the eleventh hour that God came through again, and my projected parole date would be April 18, 1998. It never fails that just before the break of dawn, something drastic would happen. It was December 15, 1997, and one of my roommates who has been locked up for a while said she was going home the next day. We had thrown her a party, and she packed all of her belongings and gave away items as well. I never thought in a million years of what would take place later on that night.

I was asleep, and all of a sudden, there was a big bang that woke everyone up out of their sleep. I jumped up so fast, and I saw my roommate lying out on the floor with blood and several teeth on the floor. It looked like something demonic, and I couldn't believe my eyes. I ran out of the dorm screaming for the officer, and I was crying so bad because it was something that I had never experienced.

Later on, that night after she was taken out to the hospital, another one of my roommates shared with me that she thought that the other roommate wanted to hurt me because she kept asking her if I was sleeping yet. She also had a shank (jailhouse knife) on the floor beside her. I always remember her telling me that everyone loves me and calls me a pretty girl, but who knew that deep down inside she was feeling some type of way about me the entire time. This taught me a valuable lesson on how people might say one thing but mean another. I was so shaken up about the entire situation, but it did not end there.

The next couple of days would be trying because we were under investigation for allegedly throwing a blanket party (beating her up with a blanket over her in order to avoid bruising) and giving her drugs. I couldn't believe that this was happening; my parole could be in jeopardy for something that we had no clue of what was going on. God once again stepped in, and the truth was revealed, and she was shipped back to Dwight for observation in the mental health unit.

It was stated that she was going to kill herself and slice me up before she did it because truth be told, she had ten more years left on her sentence. That was the worse experience of my entire time being incarcerated, and I will never forget the effect it had on the entire unit over an outright lie! Well, I made it through, and April 16 finally came. I got out early because the eighteenth was on a Sunday.

When the correction officer called my name, I knew my parents were there with my children who were now eight and six years old. I imagined how the ride home would be with so many questions that you can never be prepared for. It was a very bittersweet moment because I had met some wonderful people there who had played a significant role in my journey and a few I called my family with hopes of seeing them again once they were released, especially Ma G.

We had been together from the county with a bond that couldn't be broken. We had many trials and tribulations while being incarcerated, and we dealt with them together and with our trust in God. The time that was most trying was when she went through her chemo and radiation. She would be so tired and cry a lot but she never gave up and eventually beat that round of cancer. She had a few years left, and I really worried about her because I had always been there for her; and even though everyone loved her, I was not there to talk her through whatever she was facing. She was there for me as well, but for some reason, I always had to be the strong one because if I broke down, the other people would too.

This had nothing to do with me but the God that lived in me. I never want to take credit for the things that God has done for me. I know that He loves me and always believes that I am chosen. I gave away everything that I had in my possession except for my TV because there were so many people in there who did not have family and support and would appreciate anything.

I would sometimes feel so bad for people who never got mail or money that I would wait until later to get it from the C/O. I would often buy the food but was never the Crock-Pot cook, so others would always prepare the meals for me and my roommates. One thing that I noticed was that people would share with individuals who were known for getting some money on their books. I felt that was a little selfish, so I would share with less fortunate people.

I have been an empath my entire life, and for the most part, I would not trade it for anything. It's a gift! I was so happy to leave that place and never looked back. April 16, 1998 was one of the happiest days of my life. My children, even though they were still confused on what had actually happened to their mother, were excited to have me home. It was all love for the Boyd family. I had figured it would take some adjusting to, but everything was working out for my good; and just like the enemy does, he set a trap for me. He continued to send distraction because he wanted to finish the job; he wanted me dead and hopeless. He wanted me to forget what God had done for me and not fulfill my purpose.

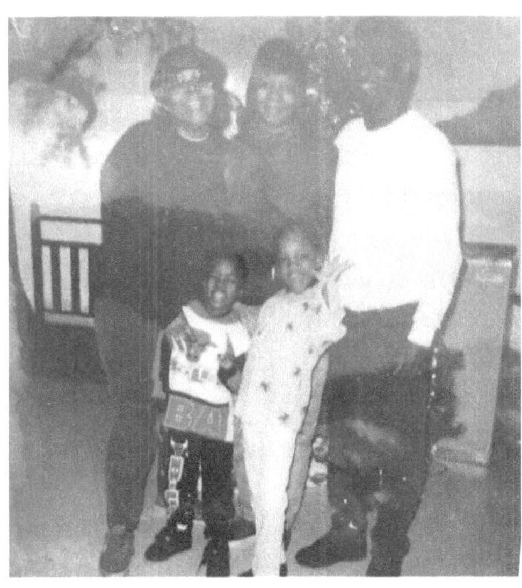

More Lessons to Learn

I was on the right track, searching for jobs, spending time with my family, and getting readjusted to society. I let my guards down, and before you know it, I began hanging out with a different group of people who still had ties to the street life, hustling and using on occasion. I was becoming frustrated with the system and could not find a job. I was free but still locked up. I had been to prison and learned a lot about how the system worked, but I still had so much to learn about our unjust system.

I was hanging with these ladies who were very good *boosters* (stealing clothes). I never cared for that lifestyle, but on a few occasions, I would return a few items for them. I was safe, and what could really go wrong? Jail had never crossed my mind, especially since I was not the one stealing. I was eighteen months into my parole, and I had gone into the store with a couple of people, and I was there to basically look out. They were leaving the store and got caught with some items, and because I was with them, they grabbed me as well. I did not have anything but some perfume in my hand, and because of that, I was charged with a thirty-dollar bottle of perfume that I never stole or was even by the door with. When I asked why they were messing with me, they said it looked like I could outrun the security guard. I was not worried because I knew that this was some bogus stuff, and the people I was with had already told me they would throw it out and that most likely the people from the store would not show up for court.

Well, as they predicted, no one showed up, and the cases were thrown out for the people who took the items. But you won't believe what happened to me. God was going to show me that this was not the life for me. The state's attorney had not only picked up the case, but they also made it a felony due to my background! I was in total disbelief, and because I was on parole, I did not have a bond.

This had to be a dream. I called my parents and told them the truth. My mom had no sympathy and told me that she did the first time with me, but she was done, and she stood on that. My brother and dad were still by my side, and as I tried to explain to them about the system, deep down inside, I figured they were still disappointed because I had made bad decisions once again. They were very supportive, but I was angry at the system and most of all at myself.

On my second court appearance, the state offered me eighteen months of IDOC, and I lost it. Did they actually think that I would take time for something that I did not do? It was at that time that I knew once again that this was a blessing in disguise, and I was being redirected before something much worse would have happened. I might be a lot of things, but I am not confused about God's love for me even when it looks like a punishment. He punishes me in order for me to correct the behaviors that I am exhibiting and because He loves me so very much. He always has something so much better for us than we can ever imagine.

Anyway, I quickly rejected that offer and knew that I would be here for as long as it took for God's favor to take over. One thing about me is that it does not matter how bad things are looking in life, my faith always allows me to trust in God, and He has not failed me yet. The criminal court system was created to break our people, and if a person is not grounded by God, it will do just that! Many people accept plea deals, thinking they are coming out on top; but in all reality, the cop-outs are more convictions for the state.

I had talked to a few people, and they suggested that I ask for TASC probation, which was a substance abuse treatment alternative; and at this point, I would go for anything besides a trip back downstate. On my next court date, we requested an evaluation for TASC because the judge was a treatment judge, and we felt more than likely that she would agree. She did inform me that individuals with violent backgrounds didn't qualify for the program, but she approved the evaluation.

It was at that point that I knew God had the final say, and my faith would move mountains. It took over a month for me to get my evaluation, and they said that was quick. Quick to who? These few months were worse than the years I spent locked up, and I was definitely learning valuable lessons about the choices I made and how my thinking becomes irrational when it comes to my loyalty and the issues of the heart. That had been my problem in life, trusting people and putting their happiness before my own. It can also be known as being a people pleaser. When I no longer felt good on the inside, it reflected on my outward behavior.

The evaluation went well, and the counselor recommended intensive outpatient treatment and shared that he hopes the judge agrees because they don't usually accept *violent backgrounds*. This was a case where "if God is for me, then who can be against me" applies. I was not worried at all. I just didn't know how long it would be before I went back to court. A couple of weeks later, which was in the middle of December 1999, I was scheduled for court and went to the bullpen that everyone goes to for court only for them to tell me that my court date was continued.

In the process of all of this confusion, I saw a lady from my community who said, "I'm sorry for your loss," and I had no idea what she was talking about. She told me that my sister-in-law who had been fighting lupus for a long time had passed away. I was not married, but common law would be a yes. Regardless of the situation, she was my sister and always will be! Everything happens for a reason, and the reason for the court date mix-up was bigger than me, and God allowed me to find out about Bren passing away.

I was so upset. My parents never told me anything because they always told me I was too emotional. In this case, that made things worse, and I was low in my spirits for quite some time. I blamed myself for being locked up and could not get past it. I had missed the funeral, and I only have to believe that it was all for my good. I still think about it to this day. She was always supportive of me, and she always spent time with my children and would buy them outfits to match their cousins. She was one of the most selfless people that I ever met. She would be drained from dialysis yet still would come to visit me. I love her, and I miss her so very much. I never forget when a person is good to me; she was that and some.

My mom really didn't let my children go with many people, but she never had a problem with Bren. The remaining days at the county were days to remember. My court date was set for January 13, which meant that I would be in Cook County Jail during the holidays and the New Year. I was full of pain and anger! What was something that I thought would be an overnight stay in lockup for nothing turned out to be the four longest months of my life! It was finally here, and even though I believed things would work out for my good, there was a doubt in the back of my head about getting probation on top of parole. Plus, since the beginning of this mess, how the system works had been up in the air.

The verdict was in, and the judge had *agreed* with TASC probation, and I would be going home sometime that night. God had prevailed again, and my faith worked. I was so grateful; I didn't care what I needed to do or how long it took. The lesson was learned! I had found myself once again and learned the real meaning of "birds of the same feather, flock together." I had vowed to myself that I would come first and stay focused at all times. I learned that some things are not for me, and as long as I continued to try to fit in with the in-crowd and be a people pleaser, there would be consequences to follow. I learned that learning to love myself was the greatest gift of all. The greatest lesson that I learned was that God knows *best*, and I know less. He had carried me all of these years; even in my darkest hours, things were working for my good.

The Journey Continued

For the next couple of years, I would be on intensive probation as well as parole. I had to see my probation officer whose office was the next block from my home. On the first day that we met, I was really mean trying to intimidate her, and she set me straight. She checked me and put me in my place. She set the rules straight and gave me her expectations of what was required which consisted of random drug drops, completing an intensive outpatient program, twelve-step meetings, and reporting in person monthly.

We bumped heads for the first couple of months because I was just angry at the rejection I was receiving in my job search. I then went on to complete the treatment portion of IOP and knew that I had to be there for a while in order to complete the program and satisfy my probation. I had already been applying to universities in order to obtain my bachelor's degree. I didn't want anything to interfere with my probation, so I waited until I completed aftercare as well before I registered for school.

I started school in the fall of 2000 and never looked back. The more I continued to grow and change, the relationship between me and my probation officer got much better. We got so close that I would check in weekly by phone and my monthly visit. She always was bragging about me, and because of my positive progress, she decided to let me off earlier than anticipated. That must have encouraged my parole agent as well because he discharged me too. My relationship with Mary T. (probation officer) was so special to me that I called her monthly for years after I was done with probation and would go fill her in on the things I was doing with my life.

God has been good to me, and I met a lot of wonderful people in the program while making the required meetings that I had to attend for probation. It was funny going to meetings for AA, and I had never really cared for alcohol and for anything else for that much. I was in a dark place when I made the decision to experiment with drugs, so it was not any process. I went straight to the drug at that time, and I hated it, so I couldn't relate to a lot of things. All I know was that I didn't have to deal with reality! What I did relate to was that I had experienced a traumatic situation and was angry at the world.

It seemed like in my life, I always chose to go big or go home; so when things happened to me, it was out of the norm and *big*! I had major consequences, and He never wasted time letting me know. What He did do was snatch me out of trouble whenever I got in over my head. Alcohol almost killed my dad, and hard drugs were never my thing, so it was pretty simple not using drugs or alcohol, and I continued to surround myself with positive people.

All for My Good

I continued with my educational journey for many years obtaining two master's of arts degrees and working in social services (twenty-plus years) as a certified alcohol and drug counselor. They were the only people who would hire me at the time, and so I adapted like I did with everything else. I found out early in life that God wouldn't put anything on me that I couldn't take. He had placed positive individuals in my path to plant seeds that I would need in years to come in order to keep me focused and my faith strong.

As I look back over the entire ordeal of my twenties, I believe that God had worked everything together for my good, and He continues to do it. There are many things that I do not understand and probably never will; what I do know is that through it all, things could have been much worse. I have a lot of gratitude for my upbringing with the morals and values my parents instilled in me; they had planted seeds that would last a lifetime and allow me to survive the path that I chose to take and come out on top because, no matter how much time or how many times I failed, I never gave up.

There are so many hopes and dreams that I planned on achieving, but now instead of me making plans, I trust God's plan for my life and know that it will be more than I can ever imagine. Sometimes, I sit back and wonder, *What if I made different choices in high school?* I will never know, and I might not have met all the wonderful people who played such significant roles in my life. Most of all, I wouldn't have met God at 26th and California (Cook County Jail) when I got there. He had been with me all of my life, He just introduced

Himself to me at the right time and made sure He had my attention with no distractions. I now can truly say, I never saw it, but it all was for my good!

About the Author

Trenesha S. Boyd is a daughter, sister, mother, community advocate, motivational speaker, mentor, author, and formerly incarcerated person. She loves to learn new things, and education is very important to her. She has two master's degrees (community counseling and gerontology from Concordia University in Chicago). She is a certified drug and alcohol counselor who has worked in the field of social service for over twenty years. She loves her family and have learned that supporting others can be a motivating factor when faced with many life's lessons. She is CEO of I Care Too, a not-for-profit focusing on empowerment and support services. Her faith in God has carried her through some of the darkest times in her life, and she never stopped believing that everything would work out for her good! Trenesha has made her assignment to be the beacon of hope for those who might not see the light at the end of the tunnel. She looks for the good in every situation as a chance to grow and help someone. She has the gift of empathy that always allows her to put herself in someone else's shoes before making any judgment. Simplicity is her key, and she stands on the "golden rule," treating people how she wants to be treated.

www.ingramcontent.com/pod-product-compliance
Lightning Source LLC
Chambersburg PA
CBHW020855160726
47993CB00004B/1662